# Air Fryer

# Cookbook

*Crispy, Quick, and Delicious Air Fryer Oven Recipes for People On a Budget*

## Mary Carton

Legal Disclaimer

The information contained in this book and its contents is not designed to replace any form of medical or professional advice; and is not meant to replace the need for independent medical, financial, legal, or other professional advice or services that may be required. The content and information in this book have been provided for educational and entertainment purposes only.

The content and information contained in this book have been compiled from sources deemed reliable, and they are accurate to the best of the Author's knowledge, information, and belief. However, the Author cannot guarantee its accuracy and validity and therefore cannot be held liable for any errors and/or omissions. Further, changes are periodically made to this book as needed. Where appropriate and/or necessary, you must consult a professional (including but not limited to your doctor, attorney, financial advisor, or other such professional) before using any of the suggested remedies, techniques, and/or information in this book.

Upon using this book's contents and information, you agree to hold harmless the Author from any damages, costs, and expenses, including any legal fees potentially resulting from the application of any of the information in this book. This disclaimer applies to any loss, damages, or injury caused by the use and application of this book's contents, whether directly or indirectly, whether for breach of contract, tort, negligence, personal injury, criminal intent, or under any other circumstance.

You agree to accept all risks of using the information presented in this book.

You agree that by continuing to read this book, where appropriate and/or necessary, you shall consult a professional (including but not limited to your doctor, attorney, financial advisor, or other such professional) before using any of the suggested remedies, techniques, or information in this book.

# Table of Contents

# INTRODUCTION

## Breathtaking Tips And Tricks

If this is your first time using the Vortex Oven, these tips will greatly help you during your early days overcome a lot of obstacles and prepare amazing foods!

- If you are using the Rotisserie accessory, make sure to place your food before touching the "START" button on the touch control panel.

- Except for rotisserie food, though, most of the other foods will give you amazing results if you place food in a pre-heated oven. To do this, simply press the "START" button and wait until the appliance shows "Add Food," which will indicate that the appliance is ready to start cooking.

- If you are looking for a fine crisp and golden fry, all you have to do is soak your potato sticks in cold water for 15 minutes, after 15 minutes, pat them dry and spray with a bit of oil before placing them into your Air Fryer oven.

- Make sure to "Flip" your food whenever your Air Fryer shows "Turn Food," this will ensure that both sides of your food are cooking well.

- They prevent the buildup of excess steam, always make sure to pat moist food dry before placing them into your Air Fryer Oven.

- The perfect way to season your meals would be to spray them with just a little bit of cooking oil. It will help to stick the seasoning to the body.

- If you plan on baking something like pie, cookie, or cake, always make sure to cover the dish with an oven-safe lid or foil to ensure that the food does not get burnt, and the topside is saved from overcooking.

## Some Mistakes To Avoid

While using the appliance, there are some very common mistakes that people tend to make early on below some three very crucial mistakes that you should avoid making.

- Air Fryer Oven uses air to cook meals while on Air Fry food, therefore it requires enough room to "Breathe" or suck in air to cook meals properly. Therefore, you must keep the appliance in a place where it has enough breathing room.
- Always try to use baking trays or dishes that are of lighter colors. Extremely dark colors such as black will cause the tray itself to absorb more heat. This might result in uneven cooking, and the lower part of your meal might remain uncooked.
- Always make sure to keep your Air Fryer disconnected when not in use. The Air Fryer takes a minimal amount of time to heat up, so you won't have to keep it connected for hours to heat it!

# Frequently Asked Questions

Below is a set of the most common questions that might come to your mind while using the appliance for the first time!

## Can Air Fryer cause cancer?

So far, there have been no reports explicitly showing that Air Fryer might cause cancer. Despite some people claiming that it emits magnetic rays or chemicals, they are complete lies.

## Can Air Fryer make good and crispy meals?

One of the main selling points of an Air Fryer is that it can make extremely crunchy and delicious meals while being healthy. So can it cook crispy meals? Yes, it most definitely can!

## Is it possible to add liquid to Air Fryer?

As long as you are just marinating your meals, it's fine. But you should not add a large amount of liquid. However, some recipes might call you to add a bit of water from time to time.

# RECIPES

## Morning Fiesta Potato

**Serving: 3**

**Prep Time: 10 minutes**

**Cook Time: 25 minutes**

**Ingredients:**

- 1 cup new potatoes
- Scallions
- 1 teaspoon hidden valley Ranch Fiesta powder
- Non-stick spray

## Directions:

**1.** Arrange drip pan in the bottom of the Vortex Air Fryer Oven cooking chamber

**2.** Spray the basket of the air fryer with non-stick spray

**3.** Sprinkle evenly with the powder

**4.** Slice potatoes into three or four slices for each potato

**5.** Place your air fryer at 180 degrees for 10 minutes in "AIR FRY" mode

**6.** Shake the potatoes and flip them when "TURN FOOD" is shown

**7.** Cook them for 15 minutes more

**8.** Serve and enjoy!

## Nutritional Contents:

- Calories: 100
- Fat: 2g
- Carbohydrates: 19g
- Protein: 2g

# The Awesome Cup-A-Ham

**Serving: 4**

**Prep Time: 10 minutes**

**Cook Time: 4 minutes**

**Ingredients:**

- 2 cups cream cheese
- 2 eggs
- 1 pack stevia
- ½ teaspoon Cinnamon

## Directions:

**1.** Arrange drip pan in the bottom of the Vortex Air Fryer Oven cooking chamber

**2.** Preheat your air fryer to 330 degrees F in "AIR FRY" mode

**3.** Place the eggs and stevia in a bowl

**4.** Whisk until stevia is dissolved

**5.** Add the cream cheese and cinnamon to eggs

**6.** Whisk until smooth

**7.** Ladle the quarter of the batter into the air fryer

**8.** Cook for 2 minutes at 330 degrees F

**9.** Flip the pancake and then cook for 2 minutes more

**10.** Repeat the process

**11.** Serve and enjoy!

## Nutritional Contents:

- Calories: 329
- Fat: 30g
- Carbohydrates: 6g
- Protein: 10g

# Bacon-Wrapped Asparagus

**Serving: 4**

**Prep Time: 10 minutes**

**Cook Time: 20 minutes**

**Ingredients:**

- 1 bunch of asparagus
- 4 slices streaky bacon
- 1 tablespoon brown sugar
- 1 and ½ tablespoons olive oil
- 1 teaspoon brown sugar
- Garlic pepper seasoning

## Directions:

**1.** Arrange drip pan in the bottom of the Vortex Air Fryer Oven cooking chamber

**2.** Preheat your air fryer to 400 degrees F for 8 minutes in "AIR FRY" mode

**3.** Trim the asparagus to your desired length

**4.** Take a bowl and add oil, garlic pepper, sugar to make a mixture

**5.** Coat the asparagus with the mix

**6.** Wrap one piece of bacon with an asparagus stalk

**7.** To secure the wrap poke a toothpick

**8.** Place all the wraps in the basket in your Vortex Air Fryer

**9.** Cook for 8 minutes

**10.** Serve and enjoy!

## Nutritional Contents:

- Calories: 178
- Fat: 14g
- Carbohydrates: 9g
- Protein: 48g

# Cheesy Air Sticks

**Serving: 6**

**Prep Time: 10 minutes**

**Cook Time: 7-8 minutes**

**Ingredients:**

- 6 cheese sticks, snake-sized
- ¼ cup parmesan cheese, grated
- 2 eggs
- 1 tablespoon Italian seasoning
- ¼ cup flour, whole wheat
- ¼ tablespoon rosemary, grounded
- 1 tablespoon garlic powder

## Directions:

**1.** Arrange drip pan in the bottom of the Vortex Air Fryer Oven cooking chamber

**2.** Take cheese sticks and set aside

**3.** Take a shallow bowl and beat eggs into the bowl

**4.** Mix cheese, flour, and seasonings in another bowl

**5.** Roll the cheese sticks in the eggs and then in the batter

**6.** Now do the process again till the sticks as well coated

**7.** Place them in the basket of air fryer

**8.** Cook for 6-7 minutes at 370 F in "AIR FRY" mode

**9.** Serve and enjoy!

## Nutritional Contents:

- Calories: 50
- Fat: 2g
- Carbohydrates: 3g
- Protein: 2g

# Crazy Ratatouille

**Serving: 4**

**Prep Time: 10 minutes**

**Cook Time: 10-30 minutes**

**Ingredients:**

- ½ cup zucchini
- 1 yellow pepper
- 2 tomatoes
- 1 onion, peeled
- 1 garlic clove, crushed
- 2 teaspoons dried herbs
- Fresh ground black pepper
- 1 tablespoon olive oil

## Directions:

**1.** Arrange drip pan in the bottom of the Vortex Air Fryer Oven cooking chamber

**2.** Preheat your Air Fryer to 392 degrees F in "AIR FRY" mode

**3.** Cut zucchini, bell pepper, tomatoes and onion in small cubes

**4.** Take a bowl and mix in garlic, herbs, ½ teaspoon salt, season with pepper, stir in olive oil

**5.** Place bowl in basket and slide into Air Fryer

**6.** Cook for 15 minutes, stir vegetables once when the "Turn Food" mode shows

Stir well and enjoy it!

## Nutritional Contents:

- Calories: 421
- Fat: 24g
- Carbohydrates: g
- Protein: 10g

# Pineapple With Honey And Coconut

**Serving: 4**

**Prep Time: 10 minutes**

**Cook Time: 10-30 minutes**

**Ingredients:**

- ½ small, fresh pineapples
- 1 tablespoon honey
- ½ tablespoon lemon juice
- 1 tablespoon ground coconut
- ¼ ice cream sorbet

Baking paper as needed

## Directions:

**1.** Arrange drip pan in the bottom of the Vortex Air Fryer Oven cooking chamber

**2.** Preheat your Instant Vortex Air Fryer to 392 degrees F in "AIR FRY" mode, line bottom of the basket with baking paper

**3.** Cut pineapple lengthwise into eight pieces, remove the peel with eyes alongside the woody trunk

**4.** Take a bowl and mix in lemon juice and honey, brush pineapple pieces with the mixture. Transfer to the basket. Sprinkle coconut over it

**5.** Push to Air Fryer and cook for 12 minutes

Serve and enjoy some ice cream.

## Nutritional Contents:

- Calories: 80
- Fat: 5g
- Carbohydrates: 0g
- Protein: 7g

# Awesome Oven Mac And Cheese

**Serving: 6**

**Prep Time: 10 minutes**

**Cook Time: 10 minutes**

**Ingredients:**

- 1 cup elbow macaroni
- ½ cup broccoli
- ½ cup warmed milk
- 1 and ½ cheddar cheese, grated
- Salt and pepper to taste
- 1 tablespoon parmesan cheese, grated

## Directions:

**1.** Arrange drip pan in the bottom of the Vortex Air Fryer Oven cooking chamber

**2.** Pre-heat your Fryer to 400 degrees F in "AIR FRY" mode

**3.** Take a pot and add water, allow it to boil

**4.** Add macaroni and veggies and broil for about 10 minutes until the mixture is Al Dente

**5.** Drain the pasta and vegetables

**6.** Toss the pasta and veggies with cheese

**7.** Season with some pepper and salt and transfer the mixture to your Fryer

**8.** Sprinkle some more parmesan on top and cook for about 15 minutes.

**9.** Allow it to cool for about 10 minutes once done

**10.** Enjoy!

## Nutritional Contents:

- Calories: 180
- Fat: 11g
- Carbohydrates: 14g
- Protein: 6g

# Complete Baked Ramekin Egg

**Serving: 2**

**Prep Time: 10 minutes**

**Cook Time: 10 minutes**

**Ingredients:**

- 1 whole egg
- 2 streaky bacon
- 1 English muffin
- Salt and pepper to taste

## Directions:

**1.** Arrange drip pan in the bottom of the Vortex Air Fryer Oven cooking chamber

**2.** Preheat your oven to 180 degrees F in "AIR FRY" mode

**3.** Cook bacon in a skillet over medium-high heat (with a little bit of oil)

**4.** Cut bacon into small pieces and divide them equally amongst two ramekins

**5.** Dice tomatoes and add them to the ramekins

**6.** Add a tablespoon of milk onto each ramekin

**7.** Crack an egg into each ramekin

**8.** Season both with salt and pepper

**9.** Sprinkle ½ teaspoon parmesan into ramekins

**10.** Place ramekins into Air Fryer cooking basket and cook for 7 minutes

**11.** Serve and enjoy!

## Nutritional Contents:

- Calories: 200
- Fat: 118g
- Carbohydrates: 13g
- Protein: 7g

# Straight-Up Morning Bagels

**Serving: 3**

**Prep Time: 10 minutes**

**Cook Time: 12 minutes**

**Ingredients:**

- 1 cup all-purpose flour
- 2 teaspoons baking powder
- Salt, to taste
- 1 cup plain Greek Yogurt
- 1 egg, beaten
- 1 tablespoon water
- 1 tablespoon sesame seeds
- 1 teaspoon coarse salt

## Directions:

**1.** Take a large bowl and mix in flour, baking powder, and salt

**2.** Add yogurt and mix well until you have a nice doughy ball

**3.** Place dough onto a lightly floured surface and cut into 4 equal-sized balls

**4.** Roll each ball into a 7-8-inch rope then join ends to make a shape of a bagel

**5.** Place 2 bagels onto a cooking tray

**6.** Take a small bowl and add egg, water, and mix well. Brush bagels with the egg mixture evenly. Sprinkle sesame seeds and salt on top

**7.** Arrange drip pan in the bottom of the Vortex Air Fryer Oven cooking chamber, select Air Fry mode and cook for 12 minutes at 330 degrees F. Make sure not to change position when "Turn Food" is shown.

**8.** Serve and enjoy once done.

## Nutritional Contents:

- Calories: 188
- Fat: 3g
- Carbohydrates: 29g
- Protein: 9g

# Avocado Cups And Eggs

**Serving: 2**

**Prep Time: 10 minutes**

**Cook Time: 10 minutes**

**Ingredients:**

- 2 cooked bacon slices, crumbled
- Salt and pepper to taste
- 2 large whole eggs
- 1 avocado, halved and pitted

**Directions:**

1. Carefully, scoop out about 2 teaspoons of flesh from each avocado half.
2. Crack 1 egg in each avocado half and sprinkle with salt and black pepper.
3. Press "Power Button" of Air Fry Oven and turn the dial to select the "Air Roast" mode.
4. Press the Time button and again turn the dial to set the cooking time to 10 minutes. Now push the Temp

button and rotate the dial to set the temperature at 375 degrees F.

5. Press the "Start/Pause" button to start.

6. When the unit beeps to show that it is preheated, open the lid and line the "Sheet Pan" with a lightly, grease piece of foil.

7. Arrange avocado halves into the "Sheet Pan" and insert it in the oven.

8. Top each avocado half with bacon pieces and serve.

## Nutritional Contents:

- Calories: 300
- Fat: 26g
- Carbohydrates: 9g
- Protein: 10g

# Cinnamon Flavored Classic French Toast

**Serving: 3**

**Prep Time: 10 minutes**

**Cook Time: 5 minutes**

**Ingredients:**

- 4 bread slices
- 1/8 teaspoon ground cinnamon
- 1/8 teaspoon vanilla extract
- 2 teaspoons olive oil
- 3 tablespoons sugar
- ¼ cup whole milk
- 2 whole eggs

**Directions:**

1. In a large bowl, mix all the ingredients except bread slices.
2. Coat the bread slices with egg mixture evenly.
3. Press "Power Button" of Air Fry Oven and turn the dial to select the "Air Fry" mode.
4. Press the Time button and again turn the dial to set the cooking time to 6 minutes. Now push the Temp

button and rotate the dial to set the temperature at 390 degrees F.

5.  Press the "Start/Pause" button to start.

6.  When the unit beeps to show that it is preheated, open the lid and lightly, grease the sheet pan.

7.  Arrange the bread slices into "Air Fry Basket" and insert it in the oven.    Flip the bread slices once halfway through.   Serve warm.

## Nutritional Contents:

- Calories: 288
- Fat: 10g
- Carbohydrates: 20g
- Protein: 8g

# Simple Pickled Toast

**Serving: 3**

**Prep Time: 10 minutes**

**Cook Time: 5 minutes**

**Ingredients:**

- ¼ cup parmesan cheese, grated
- 2 tablespoons Branston pickle
- 2 tablespoons unsalted butter, soft
- 4 bread slices, toasted

**Directions:**

1. Spread butter over bread slices evenly, followed by Branston pickle.
2. Top with cheese evenly.
3. Press "Power Button" of Air Fry Oven and turn the dial to select the "Air Fry" mode.
4. Press the Time button and again turn the dial to set the cooking time to 5 minutes. Now push the Temp button and rotate the dial to set the temperature at 390 degrees F.

5.  Press the "Start/Pause" button to start.   When the unit beeps to show that it is preheated, open the lid and lightly, grease the sheet pan.

6.  Arrange the bread slices into "Air Fry Basket" and insert it in the oven.   Serve warm.

## Nutritional Contents:

- Calories: 211
- Fat: 14g
- Carbohydrates: 16g
- Protein: 5.5g

# Chicken And Zucchini Omelet

**Serving: 3**

**Prep Time: 10 minutes**

**Cook Time: 35 minutes**

**Ingredients:**

- 8 whole eggs
- ½ cup milk
- Salt and pepper to taste
- 1 cup cooked chicken, chopped
- 1 cup cheddar cheese, shredded
- ½ cup fresh chives, chopped
- ¾ cup zucchini, chopped

**Directions:**

1. In a bowl, add the eggs, milk, salt, and black pepper and beat well. Add the remaining ingredients and stir to combine.
2. Place the mixture into a greased baking pan.
3. Press "Power Button" of Air Fry Oven and turn the dial to select the "Air Bake" mode.

4. Press the Time button and again turn the dial to set the cooking time to 35 minutes.

5. Now push the Temp button and rotate the dial to set the temperature at 315 degrees F.    Press "Start/Pause" button to start.

6. When the unit beeps to show that it is preheated, open the lid.  Arrange pan over the "Wire Rack" and insert it in the oven.

7. Cut into equal-sized wedges and serve hot.

## Nutritional Contents:

- Calories: 207
- Fat: 13g
- Carbohydrates: 2g
- Protein: 10g

# Pancetta And Hot Dog Omelet

**Serving: 3**

**Prep Time: 10 minutes**

**Cook Time: 10 minutes**

**Ingredients:**

- 4 whole eggs
- ¼ teaspoon dried parsley
- ¼ teaspoon dried rosemary
- 1 pancetta slice, chopped
- 2 hot dogs, chopped
- 2 small onions, chopped

**Directions:**

1. In a bowl, crack the eggs and beat well.
2. Add the remaining ingredients and gently stir to combine.
3. Place the mixture into a baking pan.
4. Press "Power Button" of Air Fry Oven and turn the dial to select the "Air Fry" mode.
5. Press the Time button and again turn the dial to set the cooking time to 10 minutes.

6. Now push the Temp button and rotate the dial to set the temperature at 320 degrees F.

7. Press the "Start/Pause" button to start.

8. When the unit beeps to show that it is preheated, open the lid. Arrange pan over the "Wire Rack" and insert it in the oven.

9. Cut into equal-sized wedges and serve hot.

## Nutritional Contents:

- Calories: 282
- Fat: 20g
- Carbohydrates: 8g
- Protein: 20g

# Tomato Frittata

**Serving: 3**

**Prep Time: 10 minutes**

**Cook Time: 30 minutes**

**Ingredients:**

- Salt as needed
- 1 cup Gouda cheese, shredded
- ½ cup milk
- ½ cup tomatoes, chopped
- 4 whole eggs

**Directions:**

1. In a small baking pan, add all the ingredients and mix well.
2. Press "Power Button" of Air Fry Oven and turn the dial to select the "Air Fry" mode.
3. Press the Time button and again turn the dial to set the cooking time to 30 minutes. Now push the Temp button and rotate the dial to set the temperature at 340 degrees F. Press "Start/Pause" button to start.

4. When the unit beeps to show that it is preheated, open the lid. Arrange the baking pan over the "Wire Rack" and insert it in the oven.

5. Cut into 2 wedges and serve.

## Nutritional Contents:

- Calories: 247
- Fat: 16g
- Carbohydrates: 8g
- Protein: 18g

# Scallion Sausage Frittata

**Serving: 3**

**Prep Time: 10 minutes**

**Cook Time: 20 minutes**

**Ingredients:**

- Pinch of cayenne pepper
- 2 scallions, chopped
- 4 whole eggs, beaten
- ½ cup cheddar cheese, shredded
- ¼ pound cooked breakfast sausage, crumbled

**Directions:**

1. In a bowl, add the sausage, cheese, eggs, scallion, and cayenne, and mix until well combined.
2. Place the mixture into a greased baking pan.
3. Press "Power Button" of Air Fry Oven and turn the dial to select the "Air Fry" mode.
4. Press the Time button and again turn the dial to set the cooking time to 20 minutes.
5. Now push the Temp button and rotate the dial to set the temperature at 360 degrees F.

6. Press the "Start/Pause" button to start.

7. When the unit beeps to show that it is preheated, open the lid. Arrange pan over the "Wire Rack" and insert it in the oven.

8. Cut into equal-sized wedges and serve hot.

## Nutritional Contents:

- Calories: 437
- Fat: 32g
- Carbohydrates: 2g
- Protein: 30g

# Spinach And Mozzarella Muffins

**Serving: 3**

**Prep Time: 10 minutes**

**Cook Time: 12 minutes**

**Ingredients:**

- Salt and pepper to taste
- 4 teaspoons mozzarella cheese, grated
- 2 tablespoons frozen spinach, thawed
- 2 tablespoons half and half
- 2 large egg

**Directions:**

1. Grease 2 ramekins.
2. In each prepared ramekin, crack 1 egg.
3. Divide the half-and-half, spinach, cheese, salt, and black pepper, and each ramekin and gently stir to combine without breaking the yolks.
4. Press "Power Button" of Air Fry Oven and turn the dial to select the "Air Fry" mode.
5. Press the Time button and again turn the dial to set the cooking time to 10 minutes. Now push the Temp

button and rotate the dial to set the temperature at 330 degrees F.

6. Press the "Start/Pause" button to start.  When the unit beeps to show that it is preheated, open the lid.

7. Arrange the ramekins over the "Wire Rack" and insert it in the oven.

8. Serve and enjoy!

## Nutritional Contents:

- Calories: 251
- Fat: 16g
- Carbohydrates: 3g
- Protein: 22g

# Feisty Crab Sticks

**Serving: 4**

**Prep Time: 10 minutes**

**Cook Time: 10-12 minutes**

**Ingredients:**

- 20 ounces crabsticks, sliced into thin strips
- 1 teaspoon Cajun seasoning
- 2 teaspoons sesame oil

## Directions:

**1.** Season the crabsticks with sesame oil and Cajun seasoning

**2.** Cook for 10-12 minutes at 320 degrees F in "AIR FRY" mode

**3.** Serve and enjoy!

## Nutritional Contents:

- Calories: 105
- Fat: 5g
- Carbohydrates: 15g
- Protein: 9g

# Lemon Touched Green Beans

**Serving: 2**

**Prep Time: 10 minuted**

**Cook Time: 12 minutes**

### Ingredients:

- 1-pound green beans washed and de-stemmed
- 1 lemon
- Pinch of salt
- ¼ teaspoon oil

## Directions:

**1.** Add beans to your Air Fryer cooking basket

**2.** Squeeze a few drops of lemon

**3.** Season with salt and pepper

**4.** Drizzle olive oil on top

**5.** Cook for 10-12 minutes at 400 degrees F in "AIR FRY" mode

**6.** Once done, serve and enjoy!

## Nutritional Contents:

- Calories: 90
- Fat: 5g
- Carbohydrates: 9g
- Protein: 2g

# Indian Onion Pakora

**Serving: 4**

**Prep Time: 10 minutes**

**Cook Time: 12 minutes**

**Ingredients:**

- 1 cup Gram Flour
- ¼ cup almond flour
- 2 teaspoons olive oil
- 4 whole onion
- 2 whole green chilies

- 1 tablespoon coriander
- ¼ teaspoon carom
- 1/8 teaspoon chili powder
- Salt as needed

**Directions:**

**1.** Slice your onion into individual slices

**2.** Chop the green chilies

**3.** Cut up the coriander into equal-sized portions

**4.** Take a bowl and add carom, turmeric powder, salt, and chili powder

**5.** Add onion, chilies, and coriander

**6.** Mix well

**7.** Add water and keep mixing until you have a dough-like consistency

**8.** Mix the dough and form balls

**9.** Pre-heat your Fryer to 392 degrees Fahrenheit in "AIR FRY" mode

**10.** Cook for 8 minutes

**11.** Make sure to keep checking after every 6 minutes to ensure that they are not burnt

**Nutritional Contents:**

- Calories: 280
- Fat: 20g
- Carbohydrates: 28g
- Protein: 8g

# All-Time Favorite Veggie Cutlet

**Serving: 4**

**Prep Time: 10 minutes**

**Cook Time: 15 minutes**

**Ingredients:**

- 7 ounces potatoes
- ½ a carrot, grated
- 2 ounces capsicum, chopped
- 2 ounces cabbage, chopped
- Salt as needed
- Panko bread crumbs
- 1 teaspoons arrowroot mixed with water

**Directions:**

**1.** Take a pot of boiling water and add potatoes

**2.** Once the potatoes are boiled, take them out and let them cool

**3.** Peel the potatoes and mash them alongside cabbage, capsicum and season the mixture with salt

**4.** Divide the mixture into 6 balls

**5.** Flatten balls into cutlet shapes

**6.** Coat each ball with arrowroot slurry and dredge them in breadcrumbs

**7.** Pre-heat your Fryer to 356 degrees F in "AIR FRY" mode

**8.** Transfer balls to your Air Fryer cooking basket and cook for 8 minutes, give them a turn and cook for 8 minutes more

**9.** Serve and enjoy!

## Nutritional Contents:

- Calories: 240
- Fat: 4g
- Carbohydrates: 46g
- Protein: 7g

# McDonald's Fish Nuggets

**Serving: 4**

**Prep Time: 10 minutes**

**Cook Time: 10 minutes**

**Ingredients:**

- 1-pound fresh cod
- 2 tablespoons olive oil
- ½ cup almond flour
- 2 large finely beaten eggs
- 1-2 cups almond meal
- Salt as needed

58

## Directions:

**1.** Preheat your Air Fryer to 388 degrees F in "AIR FRY" mode

**2.** Take a food processor and add olive oil, almond meal, salt and blend

**3.** Take three bowls and add almond flour, almond meal, beaten eggs individually

**4.** Take costs and cut them into slices of 1-inch thickness and 2-inch length

**5.** Dredge slices into flour, eggs and in crumbs

**6.** Transfer nuggets to Air Fryer cooking basket and cook for 10 minutes until golden

**7.** Serve and enjoy!

## Nutritional Contents:

- Calories: 188
- Fat: 3g
- Carbohydrates: 29g
- Protein: 9g

# Paprika Dressed Potato Roast

**Serving: 4**

**Prep Time: 10 minutes**

**Cook Time: 12 minutes**

**Ingredients:**

- 56 ounces potatoes, peeled and cubed
- 2 tablespoons spicy paprika
- 4 cups Greek yogurt
- 4 tablespoons olive oil, divided
- Salt and pepper, to taste

## Directions:

1. Preheat your air fryer to 360 degrees F in "AIR FRY" mode
2. Soak the potatoes in water
3. Let it soak for 30 minutes
4. Take a paper towel then drain and pat dry
5. Add paprika, salt, pepper and half of oil in a bowl
6. Mix them well
7. Coat the potatoes in the mixture
8. Cook in the air fryer for 20 minutes
9. Meanwhile, blend the remaining oil and yogurt
10. Season with salt and pepper
11. Serve with yogurt and enjoy!

## Nutritional Contents:

- Calories: 540
- Fat: 15g
- Carbohydrates: 25g
- Protein: 60g

# Crispy Pumpkin Seeds

**Serving: 4**

**Prep Time: 10 minutes**

**Cook Time: 50 minutes**

**Ingredients:**

- 1 and ½ cups pumpkin seeds
- Olive oil as needed
- 1 and ½ teaspoons salt
- 1 teaspoon smoked paprika

## Directions:

**1.** Cut pumpkin and scrape out seeds and flesh

**2.** Separate flesh from seeds and rinse the seeds under cold water

**3.** Bring 2 quarter of salted water to boil and add seeds, boil for 10 minutes

**4.** Drain seeds and spread them on a kitchen towel

**5.** Dry for 20 minutes

**6.** Preheat your fryer to 350 degrees F in "AIR FRY" mode

**7.** Take a bowl and add seeds, smoked paprika, and olive oil

**8.** Season with salt and transfer to your Air Fryer cooking basket

**9.** Cook for 35 minutes, enjoy it!

## Nutritional Contents:

- Calories: 270
- Fat: 21g
- Carbohydrates: 4g
- Protein: 12g

# Goat Cheese And Broccoli Salad

**Serving: 4**

**Prep Time: 10 minutes**

**Cook Time: 10 minutes**

**Ingredients:**

- 2 ounces broccoli florets
- 3 onions
- 3 and ½ ounces of goat cheese
- 4 tomatoes, sliced
- 4 bell peppers
- Cooking spray
- Salt and pepper, to taste

## Directions:

**1.** Use cooking spray to coat bell peppers, broccoli, and onions

**2.** Preheat your air fry at 360 degrees F in "AIR FRY" mode

**3.** Cook for 10 minutes

**4.** Take a salad bowl and transfer the mixture into it

**5.** Add goat cheese and tomatoes on top

**6.** Then season with pepper and salt

**7.** Serve and enjoy!

## Nutritional Contents:

- Calories: 380
- Fat: 15g
- Carbohydrates: 8g
- Protein: 50g

# Feisty Roasted Cashews

**Serving: 3**

**Prep Time: 10 minutes**

**Cook Time: 5 minutes**

**Ingredients:**

- 1 and ½ cups raw cashew nuts
- 1 teaspoons butter, melted
- Salt and pepper to taste

**Directions:**

1. In a bowl, mix all the ingredients.
2. Press "Power Button" of Air Fry Oven and turn the dial to select the "Air Fry" mode.
3. Press the Time button and again turn the dial to set the cooking time to 5 minutes.
4. Now push the Temp button and rotate the dial to set the temperature at 355 degrees F.
5. Press the "Start/Pause" button to start. When the unit beeps to show that it is preheated, open the lid.
6. Arrange the cashews in "Air Fry Basket" and insert them in the oven.
7. Shake the cashews once halfway through.

**Nutritional Contents:**

- Calories: 202
- Fat: 16g
- Carbohydrates: 11g
- Protein: 6g

# Spiced Up Carrot Fries

**Serving: 3**

**Prep Time: 10 minutes**

**Cook Time: 12 minutes**

**Ingredients:**

- Salt and pepper to taste
- ¼ teaspoon cayenne pepper
- 1 tablespoon olive oil
- 1 tablespoon fresh rosemary, chopped
- 1 large carrot, peeled and cut

**Directions:**

1. In a bowl, add all the ingredients and mix well.
2. Press "Power Button" of Air Fry Oven and turn the dial to select the "Air Fry" mode.
3. Press the Time button and again turn the dial to set the cooking time to 12 minutes. Now push the Temp button and rotate the dial to set the temperature at 390 degrees F.
4. Press the "Start/Pause" button to start.
5. When the unit beeps to show that it is preheated, open the lid.

6.  Arrange the carrot fries in "Air Fry Basket" and insert it in the oven.

## Nutritional Contents:

- Calories: 81
- Fat: 8g
- Carbohydrates: 5g
- Protein: 0.4g

# Elegant Potato Chips

**Serving: 4**

**Prep Time: 10 minutes**

**Cook Time: 30 minutes**

**Ingredients:**

- ¼ teaspoon salt
- 2 tablespoons fresh rosemary, chopped
- 1 tablespoon olive oil
- 4 small russet potatoes, sliced

**Directions:**

1. In a large bowl of water, soak the potato slices for about 30 minutes, changing the water once halfway through.
2. Drain the potato slices well and pat them dry with the paper towels.
3. Press "Power Button" of Air Fry Oven and turn the dial to select the "Air Fry" mode.
4. Press the Time button and again turn the dial to set the cooking time to 25 minutes. Now push the Temp button and rotate the dial to set the temperature at 350 degrees F.

5. Press the "Start/Pause" button to start.

6. When the unit beeps to show that it is preheated, open the lid. Arrange the potato chips in "Air Fry Basket" and insert it in the oven.

7. Toss the potato chips once halfway through.

## Nutritional Contents:

- Calories: 102
- Fat: 3g
- Carbohydrates: 18g
- Protein: 2g

# Buttery Corn Cob

**Serving: 3**

**Prep Time: 10 minutes**

**Cook Time: 20 minutes**

**Ingredients:**

- 2 tablespoons butter, soft and divided
- Salt and pepper to taste
- 2 corn on the cob

**Directions:**

1. Sprinkle the cobs evenly with salt and black pepper.
2. Then, rub with 1 tablespoon of butter.
3. With 1 piece of foil, wrap each cob.
4. Press "Power Button" of Air Fry Oven and turn the dial to select the "Air Fry" mode.
5. Press the Time button and again turn the dial to set the cooking time to 20 minutes.
6. Now push the Temp button and rotate the dial to set the temperature at 320 degrees F.
7. Press the "Start/Pause" button to start.
8. When the unit beeps to show that it is preheated, open the lid.

9. Arrange the cobs in "Air Fry Basket," insert in your oven

10.      Serve and enjoy once the timer runs out

## Nutritional Contents:

- Calories: 186
- Fat: 12g
- Carbohydrates: 20g
- Protein: 3g

# Cauliflower Poppers

**Serving: 3**

**Prep Time: 10 minutes**

**Cook Time: 8 minutes**

**Ingredients:**

- Sat and pepper to taste
- 1 tablespoon olive oil
- ½ large head cauliflower, cut into bite-sized florets

**Directions:**

1. In a bowl, add all the ingredients and toss to coat well.
2. Press "Power Button" of Air Fry Oven and turn the dial to select the "Air Fry" mode.
3. Press the Time button and again turn the dial to set the cooking time to 8 minutes.
4. Now push the Temp button and rotate the dial to set the temperature at 390 degrees F.
5. Press the "Start/Pause" button to start. When the unit beeps to show that it is preheated, open the lid.
6. Arrange the cauliflower florets in "Air Fry Basket" and insert it in the oven.
7. Toss the cauliflower florets once halfway through.

**8.** Serve and enjoy once done!

## Nutritional Contents:

- Calories: 32
- Fat: 23g
- Carbohydrates: 2g
- Protein: 0.7g

# Broccoli Poppers

**Serving: 3**

**Prep Time: 10 minutes**

**Cook Time: 12 minutes**

**Ingredients:**

- 2 tablespoons plain yogurt
- ½ teaspoon red chili powder
- ¼ teaspoon cumin, ground
- ¼ teaspoon turmeric, ground
- Salt to taste
- 2 tablespoons chickpea flour
- 1 pound broccoli, cut into florets

**Directions:**

1. In a bowl, mix the yogurt and spices.
2. Add the broccoli and coat with marinade generously.
3. Refrigerate for about 20 minutes.
4. Press "Power Button" of Air Fry Oven and turn the dial to select the "Air Fry" mode.
5. Press the Time button and again turn the dial to set the cooking time to 10 minutes.

6. Now push the Temp button and rotate the dial to set the temperature at 400 degrees F. Press "Start/Pause" button to start.

7. When the unit beeps to show that it is preheated, open the lid.

8. Arrange the broccoli florets in "Air Fry Basket" and insert it in the oven.

9. Toss the broccoli florets once halfway through.

10. Once done, enjoy it!

## Nutritional Contents:

- Calories: 69
- Fat: 0.9g
- Carbohydrates:  12g
- Protein: 4g

# Tender Rice Flour Bites

**Serving: 3**

**Prep Time: 10 minutes**

**Cook Time: 12 minutes**

**Ingredients:**

- 1-ounce parmesan cheese, shredded
- ¾ cup of rice flour
- ½ teaspoon vegetable oil
- 6 tablespoons milk

**Directions:**

1. In a bowl, add milk, flour, oil, and cheese, and mix until smooth dough forms. Make small equal-sized balls from the dough.
2. Press "Power Button" of Air Fry Oven and turn the dial to select the "Air Fry" mode.
3. Press the Time button and again turn the dial to set the cooking time to 12 minutes.
4. Now push the Temp button and rotate the dial to set the temperature at 300 degrees F. Press "Start/Pause" button to start.

5. When the unit beeps to show that it is preheated, open the lid.

6. Arrange the balls in "Air Fry Basket" and insert them in the oven.

7. Serve and enjoy once the timer runs out!

**Nutritional Contents:**

- Calories: 148
- Fat: 3g
- Carbohydrates: 25g
- Protein: 4g

# Vortex Chicken Nuggets

**Serving: 4**

**Prep Time: 10 minutes**

**Cook Time: 10 minutes**

**Ingredients:**

- Salt and pepper as needed
- ¼ teaspoon smoked paprika
- 1 teaspoon onion powder
- 1/3 tablespoon parmesan cheese, shredded
- 1 cup breadcrumbs
- 2 large chicken breast cut into 1-inch cubes

**Directions:**

1. In a large resealable bag, add all the ingredients.
2. Seal the bag and shake well to coat completely.
3. Press "Power Button" of Air Fry Oven and turn the dial to select the "Air Fry" mode.
4. Press the Time button and again turn the dial to set the cooking time to 10 minutes. Now push the Temp button and rotate the dial to set the temperature at 400 degrees F. Press "Start/Pause" button to start.

5. When the unit beeps to show that it is preheated, open the lid.

6. Arrange the nuggets in "Air Fry Basket" and insert it in the oven.

7. Serve once done, enjoy!

## Nutritional Contents:

- Calories: 218
- Fat: 6g
- Carbohydrates: 13g
- Protein: 24g

# Spinach And Mozzarella Muffins

**Serving: 3**

**Prep Time: 10 minutes**

**Cook Time: 19 minutes**

**Ingredients:**

- ¼ cup BBQ sauce
- Salt and pepper to taste
- 1 teaspoon garlic powder
- 1 teaspoon smoked paprika
- 1 teaspoon olive oil
- 2 pounds of chicken wings

**Directions:**

1. In a large bowl, combine chicken wings, smoked paprika, garlic powder, oil, salt, and pepper and mix well.

2. Press "Power Button" of Air Fry Oven and turn the dial to select the "Air Fry" mode. Press the Time button and again turn the dial to set the cooking time to 19 minutes. Now push the Temp button and rotate the dial to set the temperature at 360 degrees F.

3. Press the "Start/Pause" button to start.

4. When the unit beeps to show that it is preheated, open the lid.

5. Arrange the chicken wings in "Air Fry Basket" and insert it in the oven.

6. After 12 minutes of cooking, flip the wings and coat with barbecue sauce evenly.

7. Once the timer runs out, enjoy!

**Nutritional Contents:**

- Calories: 468
- Fat: 18g
- Carbohydrates: 6g
- Protein: 65g

# Rosemary Beef Roast

**Serving: 3**

**Prep Time: 10 minutes**

**Cook Time: 15 minutes**

**Ingredients:**

- 2 pounds beef roast
- 1 tablespoon olive oil
- 1 medium onion
- 1 teaspoon salt
- 2 teaspoons rosemary and thyme

## Directions:

**1.** Place beef roast in Air Fryer cooking basket, rub it well with olive oil, rosemary, thyme, and onion

**2.** Arrange drip pan in the bottom of the Vortex Air Fryer Oven cooking chamber

**3.** Let the Air Fryer pre-heat to 390 degrees F using the "Air Fryer" button

**4.** Once done, place meat inside and cook for 15 minutes

**5.** Flip roast once "Turn Food" is shown

**6.** Serve and enjoy!

## Nutritional Contents:

- Calories: 290
- Fat: 14g
- Carbohydrates: 8g
- Protein: 32g

# Terrific Tarragon Beef Shank

**Serving: 3**

**Prep Time: 10 minutes**

**Cook Time: 90 minutes**

**Ingredients:**

- 2 tablespoons olive oil
- 2 pounds beef shank
- Salt and pepper to taste
- 1 onion, diced
- 2 stalks celery, diced
- 1 cup Marsala wine
- 2 tablespoons dried tarragon

## Directions:

**1.** Place beef shanks in baking pan, take a bowl and whisk in remaining ingredients

**2.** Pour over shanks

**3.** Place shanks in Air Fryer Basket

**4.** Arrange drip pan in the bottom of the Vortex Air Fryer Oven cooking chamber

**5.** Preheat your Air Fryer oven to 400 degrees F in "AIR FRY" mode

**6.** Set a timer to 90 minutes and cook at 400 degrees F

**7.** Once done, serve and enjoy

## Nutritional Contents:

- Calories: 400
- Fat: 9g
- Carbohydrates: 32g
- Protein: 30g

# Juiced Up Roasted Beef

**Serving: 3**

**Prep Time: 10 minutes**

**Cook Time: 12 minutes**

**Ingredients:**

- 2 teaspoons olive oil
- 4 pounds top round roast beef
- 1 teaspoon salt
- ¼ teaspoon fresh ground black pepper
- 1 teaspoon dried thyme
- ½ teaspoon fresh rosemary, chopped
- 3 pounds red potatoes, halved
- Olive oil, fresh ground black pepper, and salt for garnish

## Directions:

**1.** Arrange drip pan in the bottom of the Vortex Air Fryer Oven cooking chamber

**2.** Preheat your Air Fryer to 360 degrees F in "AIR FRY" mode

**3.** Rub olive oil all over the beef

**4.** Take a bowl and add rosemary, thyme, salt, and pepper

**5.** Mix well

**6.** Season the beef with the mixture and transfer the meat to your Fryer

**7.** Cook for 20 minutes

**8.** Add potatoes alongside some pepper and oil

**9.** Turn the roast alongside and add the potatoes to the basket

**10.** Cook for 20 minutes

**11.** Make sure to rotate the mixture from time to time

**12.** Cook until you have reached your desired temperature (130F for Rare, 140F for Medium and 160F for Well done)

**13.** Once done, allow the meat to cool for 10 minutes

**14.** Preheat your Air Fryer to 400 degrees F and keep cooking the potatoes for 10 minutes

**15.** Serve with the potatoes with the beef and enjoy it!

**Nutritional Contents:**

- Calories: 183
- Fat: 5g
- Carbohydrates: 10g
- Protein: 1g

# Cheesy Bacon Fries

**Serving: 4**

**Prep Time: 10 minutes**

**Cook Time: 16 minutes**

## Ingredients:

- 2 large russet potatoes, peeled and cut into ½ inch strips
- 4 slices bacon, diced
- 2 tablespoons olive oil
- 2 and ½ cups cheddar, cheese
- 3 ounces melted cream cheese
- Salt and pepper to taste

- ¼ cup scallions, chopped
- Ranch dressing if preferred

**Directions:**

**1.** Take a large bowl and mix in flour, baking powder, and salt

**2.** Bring a large pot of water to a boil.

**3.** Blanch the potatoes in the salted water for about 4 minutes and strain them in a colander

**4.** Rinse them with cold water and to remove the starch

**5.** Dry potatoes

**6.** Heat the fryer to 400° F in "AIR FRY" mode

**7.** Place the chopped bacon into your air fryer and fry for about 4 minutes; shake the basket halfway through

**8.** Drain the bacon and discard any excess grease that accumulated in the bottom of the fryer

**9.** Arrange drip pan in the bottom of the Vortex Air Fryer Oven cooking chamber

**10.** Toss the dried potato sticks with some oil and place them in the fryer basket

**11.** Fry them at 360° F for 25 minutes; shake the basket from time to time

**12.** Season fries with some salt and pepper about halfway through the cooking process

**13.** Transfer the fries from your basket to an 8-inch pan

**14.** Mix about 2 cups of cheddar cheese with the melted cream cheese

**15.** Dollop the cheese mix over the potatoes

**16.** Sprinkle some more cheddar cheese over the fries and top them with crumbled bacon

**17.** Lower the baking pan into your Air Fryer's cooking basket using a sling

**18.** Air-dry it for about 5 minutes at 340° F

**19.** Sprinkle some chopped scallions as a garnish and serve with your favorite ranch dressing

## Nutritional Contents:

- Calories: 118
- Fat: 8g
- Carbohydrates: 6g
- Protein: 5g

# Bacon And Garlic Platter

**Serving: 3**

**Prep Time: 10 minutes**

**Cook Time: 30 minutes**

**Ingredients:**

- 4 potatoes, halved and peeled
- 6 garlic cloves, unpeeled and squashed
- 4 rashers streaky bacon, roughly cut
- 2 sprigs rosemary
- 1 tablespoon olive oil

## Directions:

**1.** Take a bowl and add garlic, bacon, rosemary, and potatoes

**2.** Add oil and mix well

**3.** Arrange drip pan in the bottom of the Vortex Air Fryer Oven cooking chamber

**4.** Preheat your Air Fryer to 392 degrees F in "AIR FRY" mode

**5.** Transfer mixture to Air Fryer cooking basket and roast for 25-30 minutes

**6.** Serve and enjoy!

## Nutritional Contents:

- Calories: 240
- Fat: 14g
- Carbohydrates: 32g
- Protein: 6g

# Honey-Licious Pork Ribs

**Serving: 4**

**Prep Time: 10 minutes**

**Cook Time: 16 minutes**

**Ingredients:**

- 1-pound pork ribs
- 1 teaspoon salt
- 1 teaspoon pepper
- 1 tablespoon sugar
- 1 teaspoon ginger juice
- 1 teaspoon five-spice powder
- 1 tablespoon teriyaki sauce

- 1 tablespoon light soy sauce
- 1 garlic clove, minced
- 2 tablespoons honey
- 1 tablespoon water
- 1 tablespoon tomato sauce

**Directions:**

**1.** Prepare marinade by mixing the pepper, sugar, salt, five-spice powder, teriyaki sauce, ginger juice and mix well

**2.** Arrange drip pan in the bottom of the Vortex Air Fryer Oven cooking chamber

**3.** Rub mixture all over the pork and let it marinate for 2 hours

**4.** Preheat your Air Fryer to 350 degrees F in "AIR FRY" mode

**5.** Add ribs to your Air Fryer and cook for 8 minutes

**6.** Take a mixing bowl and add soy sauce, garlic, honey, water, and tomato sauce

**7.** Mix well

**8.** Stir fry the garlic in oil until fragrant

**9.** Transfer the Air Fried pork ribs to the pan with garlic and add sauce

**10.** Mix and enjoy!

**Nutritional Contents:**

- Calories: 300
- Fat: 22g
- Carbohydrates: 10g
- Protein: 15g

# Fierce Beef Schnitzel

**Serving:** 4

**Prep Time: 10 minutes**

**Cook Time: 12 minutes**

## Ingredients:

- 2 tablespoons olive oil
- 2 ounces breadcrumbs
- 1 whisked egg
- 1 thin beef schnitzel
- 1 lemon

**Directions:**

**1.** Arrange drip pan in the bottom of the Vortex Air Fryer Oven cooking chamber

**2.** Preheat your Air Fryer to 356 degrees F in "AIR FRY" mode

**3.** Take a bowl and add breadcrumbs, oil and mix well

**4.** Keep stirring until you have a good loose texture

**5.** Dip schnitzel into the egg and shake any excess

**6.** Dredge coat schnitzel into breadcrumbs and coat them

**7.** Layer in Fryer basket and cook for 12 minutes

**8.** Serve with a garnish of lemon

**9.** Enjoy!

**Nutritional Contents:**

- Calories: 420
- Fat: 3g
- Carbohydrates: 40g
- Protein: 33g

# Original Chimichurri Steaks

**Serving:** 4

**Prep Time: 10 minutes**

**Cook Time: 12 minutes**

**Ingredients:**

- 16 ounces skirt steak

## Chimichurri Sauce

- 1 cup parsley, chopped
- ¼ cup mint, chopped
- 2 tablespoons oregano, chopped

- 3 garlic cloves, chopped
- 1 teaspoon crushed red pepper
- 1 tablespoon cumin, grounded
- 1 teaspoon cayenne pepper
- 2 teaspoons smoked paprika
- 1 teaspoon salt
- ¼ teaspoon pepper
- ¾ cup olive oil
- 3 tablespoons red wine vinegar

## Directions:

**1.** Take a bowl and mix all of the ingredients listed under Chimichurri section and mix them well

**2.** Cut the steak into 2 pieces of 8-ounce portions

**3.** Take a resealable bag and add ¼ cup of Chimichurri alongside the steak pieces and shake them to ensure that steak is coated well

**4.** Allow it to chill in your fridge for 2-24 hours

**5.** Remove the steak from the fridge 30 minutes before cooking

**6.** Arrange drip pan in the bottom of the Vortex Air Fryer Oven cooking chamber

**7.** Pre-heat your Fryer to 390 degrees Fahrenheit in "AIR FRY" mode

**8.** Transfer the steak to your Fryer and cook for about 8-10 minutes if you are looking for a medium-rare finish

**9.** Garnish with 2 tablespoons of Chimichurri sauce and enjoy!

## Nutritional Contents:

- Calories: 300
- Fat: 18g
- Carbohydrates: 80g
- Protein: 13g

# Authentic Carrot Beefcake

**Serving: 4**

**Prep Time: 10 minutes**

**Cook Time: 60 minutes**

**Ingredients:**

- ½ pound ground pork
- 2 pounds lean ground beef
- 2 cups carrots, shredded
- 1 cup dry bread crumbs
- 1-ounce onion soup mix
- ½ cup almond milk
- 3 whole eggs, beaten

**Directions:**

1. Thoroughly mix ground beef with carrots and all other ingredients in a bowl.
2. Grease a meatloaf pan with oil or butter and spread the minced beef in the pan. Press "Power Button" of Air Fry Oven and turn the dial to select the "Bake" mode.
3. Press the Time button and again turn the dial to set the cooking time to 60 minutes.

4. Now push the Temp button and rotate the dial to set the temperature at 350 degrees F.

5. Once preheated, place the beef baking pan in the oven and close its lid. Slice and serve.

## Nutritional Contents:

- Calories: 212
- Fat: 11g
- Carbohydrates: 14g
- Protein: 17g

# Crumble-Friendly Oat Meatloaf

**Serving: 6**

**Prep Time: 10 minutes**

**Cook Time: 60 minutes**

**Ingredients:**

- Salt and pepper to taste
- 1 tablespoon Worcestershire sauce
- 1 large egg, beaten
- ½ cup onion, chopped
- ¾ Quaker oats
- 1 cup of salsa
- 2 pounds ground beef

**Directions:**

1. Thoroughly mix ground beef with salsa, oats, onion, egg, and all the ingredients in a bowl.
2. Grease a meatloaf pan with oil or butter and spread the minced beef in the pan.
3. Press "Power Button" of Air Fry Oven and turn the dial to select the "Bake" mode.

4. Press the Time button and again turn the dial to set the cooking time to 60 minutes.

5. Now push the Temp button and rotate the dial to set the temperature at 350 degrees F.

6. Once preheated, place the beef baking pan in the oven and close its lid.  Slice and serve.

## Nutritional Contents:

- Calories: 412
- Fat: 24g
- Carbohydrates: 43g
- Protein: 18g

# Delicious Beef Pesto Bake

**Serving: 4**

**Prep Time: 10 minutes**

**Cook Time: 35 minutes**

**Ingredients:**

- 25 ounces potatoes, boiled
- 14 ounces beef, minced
- 23 ounces jar tomato pasta
- 12 ounces pesto
- 1 tablespoon olive oil

**Directions:**

1. Mash the potatoes in a bowl and stir in pesto.
2. Sauté beef mince with olive oil in a frying pan until brown.
3. Layer a casserole dish with tomato pasta sauce.
4. Top the sauce with beef mince.
5. Spread the green pesto potato mash over the beef in an even layer.

6. Press "Power Button" of Air Fry Oven and turn the dial to select the "Bake" mode.

7. Press the Time button and again turn the dial to set the cooking time to 35 minutes.

8. Now push the Temp button and rotate the dial to set the temperature at 350 degrees F.

9. Once preheated, place casserole dish in the oven and close its lid.

10.        Once done, serve and enjoy!

## Nutritional Contents:

- Calories: 352
- Fat: 14g
- Carbohydrates: 15g
- Protein: 26g

# Beef And Potato Meatballs

**Serving: 4**

**Prep Time: 10 minutes**

**Cook Time: 20 minutes**

**Ingredients:**

- 1 and ½ ounces potato chips, crushed
- 1-ounce cheese, grated
- 1 pound potato, cooked and mashed
- 1 pinch salt and pepper
- 2 teaspoons curry powder
- 1 tablespoon parsley, chopped
- ½ pound beef, minced

**Directions:**

1. Thoroughly mix the beef with potato and all other ingredients in a bowl.
2. Make small meatballs out of this mixture then place them in the air fryer basket.
3. Press "Power Button" of Air Fry Oven and turn the dial to select the "Air fry" mode.

4. Press the Time button and again turn the dial to set the cooking time to 20 minutes.

5. Now push the Temp button and rotate the dial to set the temperature at 350 degrees F.

6. Once preheated, place meatballs basket in the oven and close its lid. Flip the meatballs when cooked halfway through.

7. Enjoy!

## Nutritional Contents:

- Calories: 301
- Fat: 15g
- Carbohydrates: 31g
- Protein: 28g

# Triple Colored Beef Skewers

**Serving: 4**

**Prep Time: 10 minutes**

**Cook Time: 25 minutes**

**Ingredients:**

- 1 and ¼ pounds boneless beef, diced
- Large bunch of thyme
- 2 tablespoons cider vinegar
- 16 cherry tomatoes
- 1 cup cottage cheese, cubed
- 4 tablespoon rapeseed oil
- 3 garlic cloves, minced

**Directions:**

1. Toss beef with all its thyme, oil, vinegar, and garlic.
2. Marinate the thyme beef for 2 hours in a closed container in the refrigerator. Thread the marinated beef, cheese, and tomatoes on the skewers.
3. Place these skewers in an Air fryer basket.
4. Press "Power Button" of Air Fry Oven and turn the dial to select the "Air fry" mode.

5. Press the Time button and again turn the dial to set the cooking time to 25 minutes.

6. Now push the Temp button and rotate the dial to set the temperature at 350 degrees F.

7. Once preheated, place the Air fryer basket in the oven and close its lid.

8. Flip the skewers when cooked halfway through then resume cooking.

9. Serve once the timer runs out and enjoy it!

## Nutritional Contents:

- Calories: 698
- Fat: 17g
- Carbohydrates: 26g
- Protein: 117g

# Conclusion

I cannot express how honored I am to think that you found my book interesting and informative enough to read it all through to the end.

I thank you again for purchasing this book and I hope that you had as much fun reading it as I had writing it.

I bid you farewell and encourage you to move forward in your culinary journey and pray that you find success in your quest!

CPSIA information can be obtained
at www.ICGtesting.com
Printed in the USA
BVHW061005040321
601713BV00012B/1093